WHY WE LOVE

BASEBALL

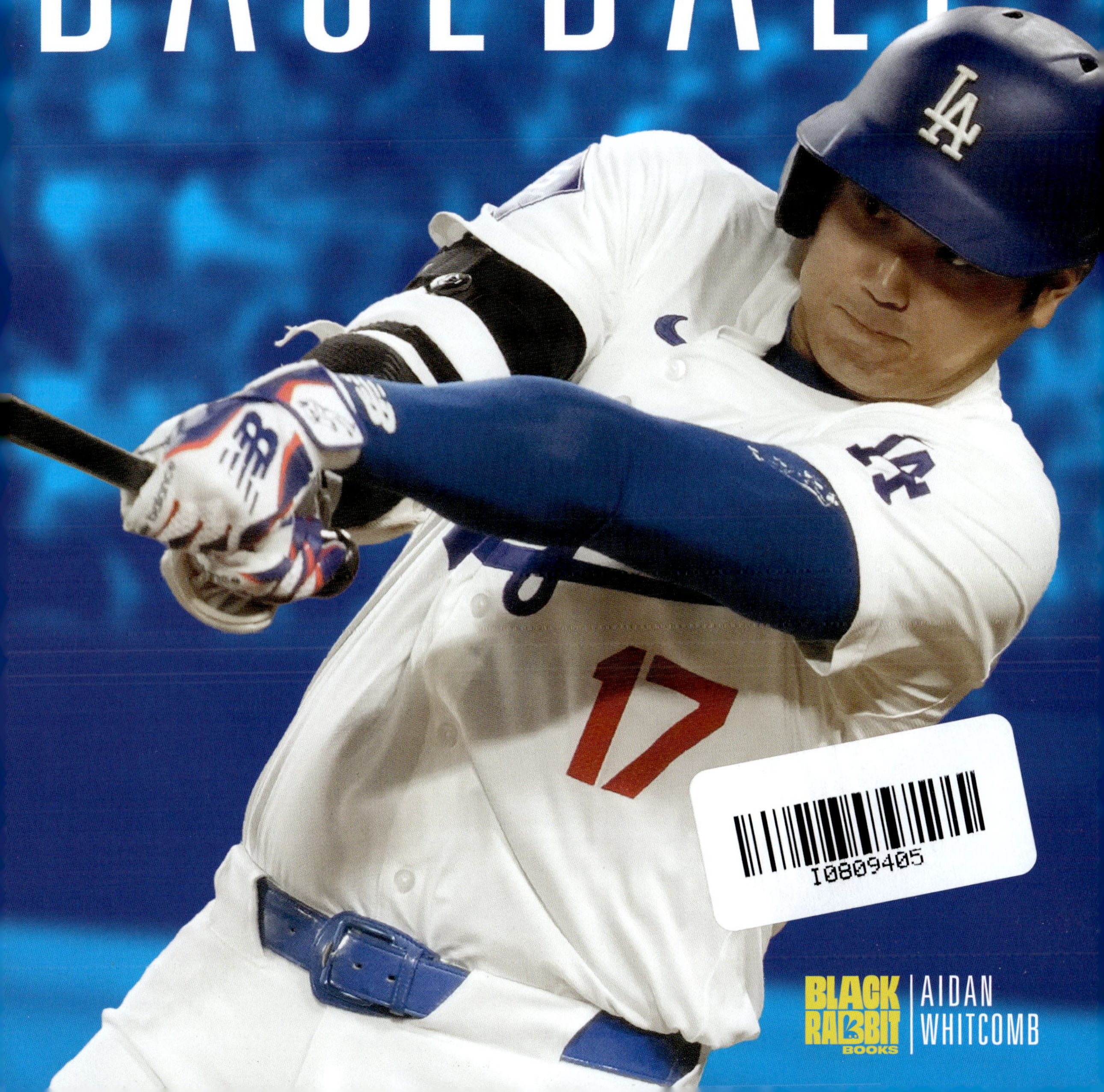

BLACK RABBIT BOOKS

AIDAN WHITCOMB

TABLE OF CONTENTS

1

America's Pastime

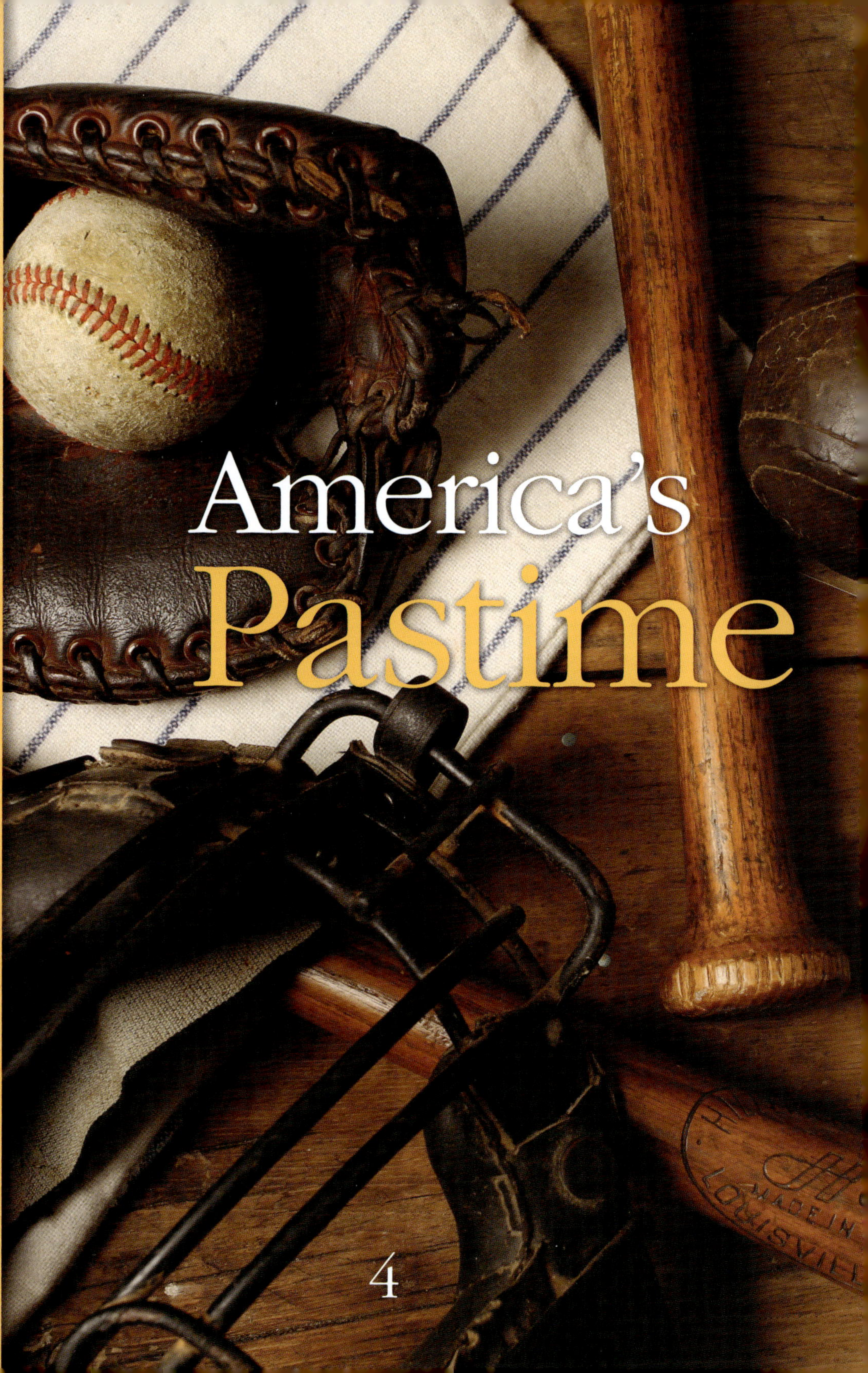

Baseball is one of America's oldest sports. It has a rich history that fans love. Many people call it "America's **Pastime**." Alexander Joy Cartwright invented baseball in 1845. Much has changed since then.

The first game was played in 1846. There were only a few fans. Today, many fans watch the games. Some Major League Baseball (MLB) teams average over 40,000 fans per game! Even more watch on TV.

Think About It

Look up baseball rules from 1846. How do they compare to today's rules?

2

Fun at the Ballpark

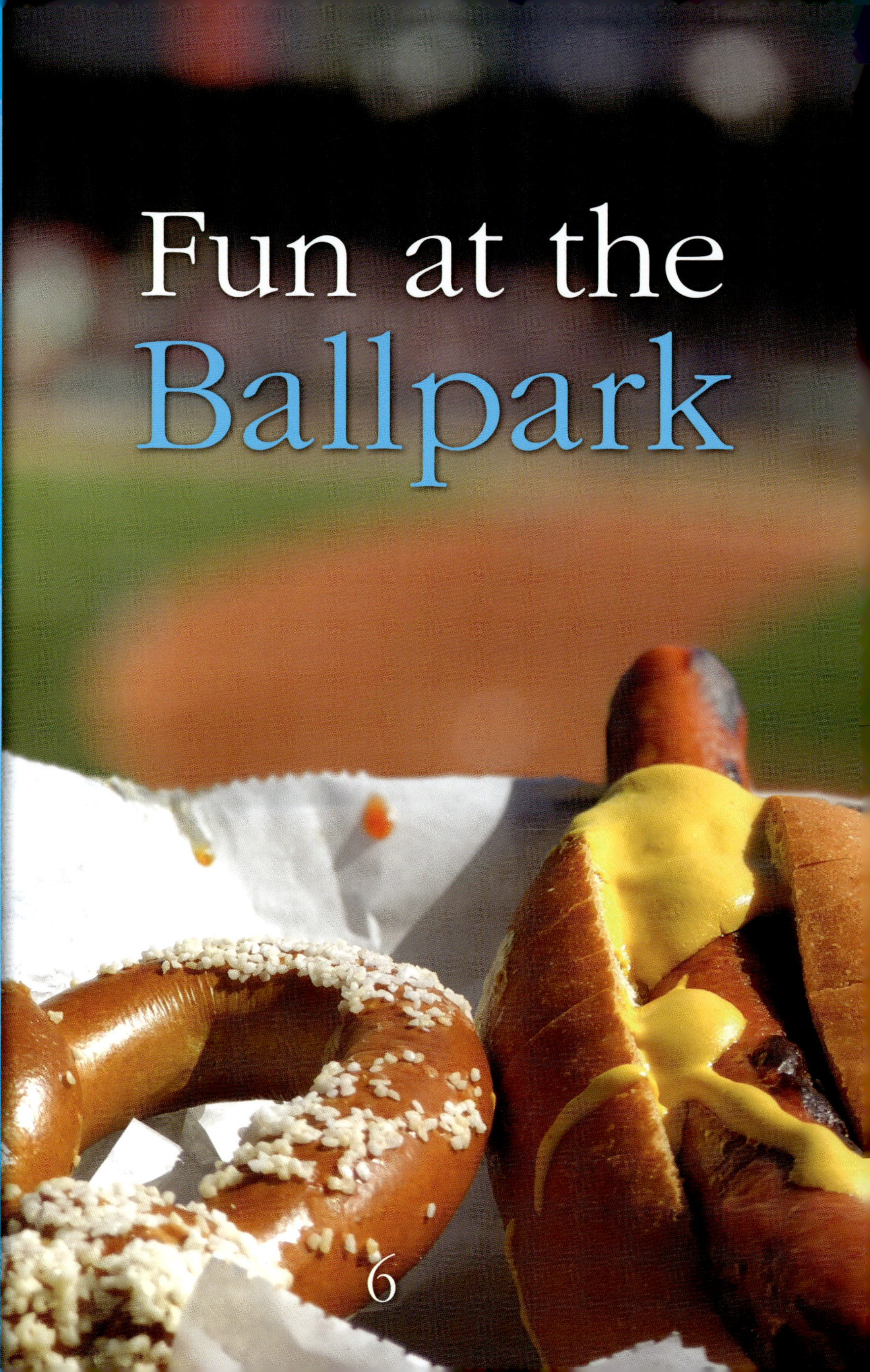

Baseball is a great sport to watch live. The whole family can enjoy it. There is so much to do at a game. There's music and food. Hot dogs and peanuts are classic ballpark snacks. And you can try to get on the dance cam! If you are lucky, you could catch a foul ball. You can bring it home as a souvenir.

It is tradition to sing "Take Me Out to the Ball Game" at games. Fans sing it during the seventh inning.

Did You Know?
Fans can collect cards of their favorite players. Most players will even sign the cards.

3

Baseball's Best

Did You Know? In 2022, Aaron Judge hit 62 home runs. Only three players have ever hit more in a season.

Aaron Judge

Many fans love the MLB's superstar players. Ronald Acuña Jr. is one of them. He plays for the Atlanta Braves. Fans love his energy. He plays with a lot of excitement. Acuña Jr. makes diving catches in center field.

Fans also enjoy watching star slugger Aaron Judge. He plays for the New York Yankees. Judge is a very large player. He is 6 foot 7 inches (2 meters) tall. He has amazing power. He blasts long home runs.

Ronald Acuña Jr.

Jarren Duran

4 Flashing the Leather

Defense is a major part of baseball. Fans love to watch great defensive plays. Infielders dive to stop the ball. Outfielders make leaping catches. Sometimes they even rob home runs!

The Gold Glove Award is given to the best defensive players. One great defensive player is Nolan Arenado. He competes for the St. Louis Cardinals. He plays third base. He has won 10 Gold Gloves Awards.

David Wright

Think About It
What do you think is more challenging? Smashing long home runs, or making crazy catches?

5 Worldwide Sport

Baseball is played all over the world. Many MLB superstars are from other countries. Roberto Clemente was a fantastic right fielder. He was from Puerto Rico. He helped make the sport popular there. He played from 1955 to 1972 for the Pittsburgh Pirates.

Shohei Ohtani is a worldwide star. He is from Japan. He plays for the Los Angeles Dodgers. Ohtani is a unique player. He is both a pitcher and a hitter. He has won two **MVP** awards!

Shohei Ohtani

Roberto Clemente

Did You Know?

Japan's Ichiro Suzuki has 4,367 career hits in professional baseball. It's the most ever!

6

All-Star Athletes

All-Star Weekend is an exciting time during baseball season. Fans vote for their favorite players. The winners go to the All-Star Game. All the best players are there. There is at least one player from each team.

Did You Know? In 2023, Vladimir Guerrero Jr. won the

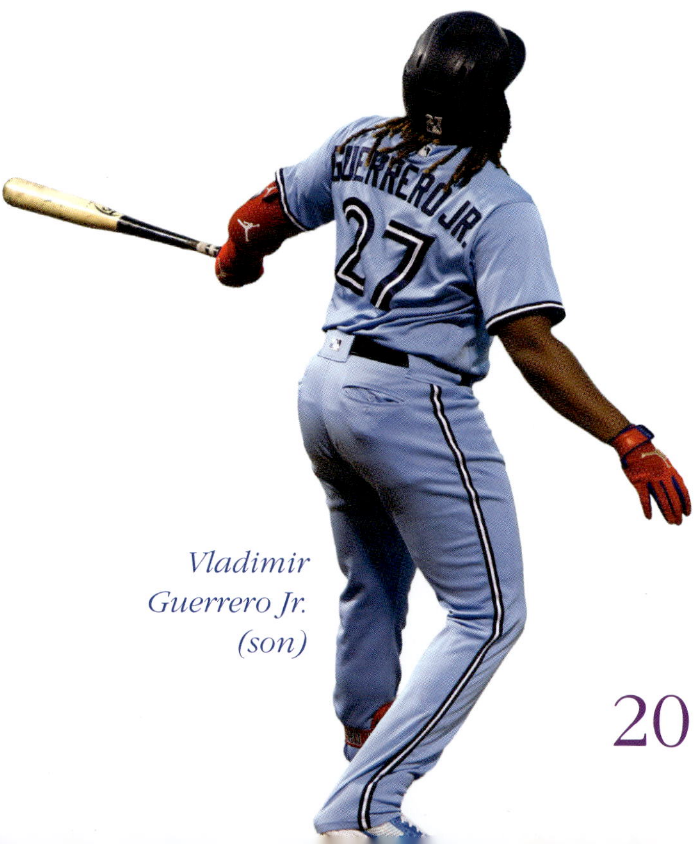

Vladimir Guerrero Jr. (son)

Some players compete in the Home Run Derby. Players hit as many home runs as possible. It is amazing how far they hit a baseball. In 2021, Juan Soto hit a 520-foot (158-meter) home run! That is the farthest ever in the Derby.

Home Run Derby. His dad also won it 16 years earlier.

Vladimir Guerrero (dad)

MORE TO EXPLORE

FANTASTIC FACTS

The New York Yankees have won the most World Series with 27 wins.

A 1952 Mickey Mantle baseball card sold for $12.6 million at an auction!

Aroldis Chapman threw a 105.8-mile-per-hour (170.3-km/h) pitch in 2010. It is the fastest in MLB history!

The longest game was 33 innings in 1981. It was a minor league game between the Pawtucket Red Sox and Rochester Red Wings.

A baseball is made with 108 stitches.

Each MLB game uses about 90 to 120 baseballs.

MORE TO EXPLORE

COOL COMPARISONS

Who's hit the longest home runs in MLB history?

BABE RUTH
(1921)
575 feet (175 m)

MICKEY MANTLE
(1953)
565 feet (172 m)

REGGIE JACKSON
(1971)
539 feet (164 m)

ADAM DUNN
(2004)
535 feet (163 m)

WILLIE STARGELL
(1978)
535 feet (163 m)

MORE TO EXPLORE

RESOURCES

Glossary

classic (KLAS-ik) Something that has been popular for a long time.

defense (DEE-fens) The players on a team who try to stop the other team from scoring.

MVP An award given to the best player in the league each season; MVP stands for most valuable player.

pastime (PAS-tahym) An activity you enjoy doing in your free time.

rob (ROB) To keep someone from getting something expected or wanted.

slugger (SLUHG-er) A batter who hits many home runs.

souvenir (SOO-veh-neer) Something kept as a reminder.

Read More

Flynn, Brendan. *The History of Baseball.* Minneapolis, MN: Jump!, Inc., 2025.

Tischler, Joe. *Shohei Ohtani.* Mankato, MN: Amicus Learning, 2025.

Index

TOP RANK is published by Black Rabbit Books, P.O. Box 227, Mankato, MN, 56002 •

• Top Rank is an imprint of Black Rabbit Books. • Designed by Danny Nanos • Photographs © Associated Press/Ashley Landis, cover, 1; Getty Images/Bettmann, 5, Daniel Shirey, 8–9, 19, Matthew J. Lee/The Boston Globe, 12–13, Rich von Biberstein/Iron Sportswire, 10–11, Tim Clayton – Corbis, 4–5; Shutterstock/Alisha Shamshad, 15, Aun-Juli Riddle, 21, Conor P. Fitzgerald, 2, 16, 20, Dan Thornberg, 3, 20, 21, 23, Debby Wong, 14, Desmond Adkins, 6, Dima Zel, 15, DJTaylor, 7, neftali, 17, nopparada samrhubsuk, 18, Snap2Art, 23, Vanessa Belfiore, cover, 1; Wikimedia Commons/Ken Lund, 13 • Printed in India.

Library of Congress Cataloging-in-Publication Data: Names: Whitcomb, Aidan, author. | Title: Why we love baseball / by Aidan Whitcomb. | Description: Mankato, MN: Top Rank, an imprint of Black Rabbit Books, [2026] | Series: Why we love sports | Includes bibliographical references and index. | Ages 8–11 | Grades 2–3 | Identifiers: LCCN 2024050034 (print) | LCCN 2024050035 (ebook) | ISBN 9781644668023 (library binding) | ISBN 9781644668344 (paperback) | ISBN 9781644668665 (ebook) | Subjects: LCSH: Basebal—-United States—Juvenile literature. | Major League Baseball (Organization)—Juvenile literature. | Classification: LCC GV867.5 .W4485 2026 (print) | LCC GV867.5 (ebook) | DDC 796.357--dc23/eng/20241121